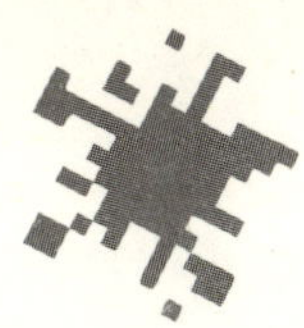

DIARY OF A MINECRAFT ZOMBIE

BOOK 22

ISBN 978-93-5471-898-4

This reprint edition May 2025

Printed In India at Shivam Offset Press, New Delhi

DIARY OF A MINECRAFT ZOMBIE

BOOK 22

THROUGH THE WORMHOLE

BY

Zack Zombie

MONDAY

'Okay, the bell is about to ring, so I want you all to finish that worksheet about the different uses for **SHOVELS** as homework. Now, remember we have our excursion to the Mob Science Museum tomorrow. If you haven't already handed in your signed permission slip, you need to give it to me tomorrow before you board the bus. And—' Ms. Bones was cut off when the school bell rang.

Nobody stuck around to hear the end of her sentence, instead packing their bags and fleeing the school.

'Duuuude,' Skelee said next to me as we walked into the hallway. 'The Mob Science Museum is gonna be **HECTIC.** I'm excited! There's gonna be buzzy things and gloopy things and exploding things!'

'If you wanna see exploding things, come over when I'm doing homework,' Creepy said sadly.

Skelee rolled his eye sockets. 'What are you most excited about?' he asked me.

'The rocket!' I answered quickly. 'The rocket is gonna be the best part. I hope it works and they show us. And I wanna see the big **BUZZY** ball of electricity too.'

'Same,' Skelee nodded. 'Big buzzy ball of electricity all the way for me.'

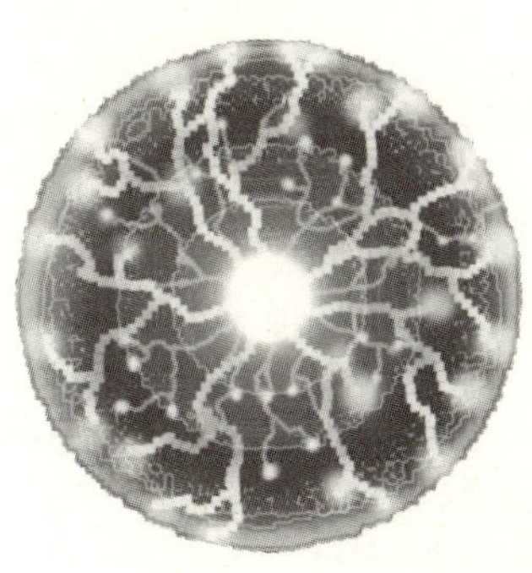

THUNK!

THUNK!

THUNK!

When I found Steve after school, he was **PUNCHING** trees again.

'Hey, dude!' I called out.

'Zombie, my man! How's it hanging?'

'Alright, I think. My mom told me to bring you some cake. She made it special for you as a thank you for trying to save her from what could have been an evil circus ringmaster.'

Steve and me thought Mom had been kidnapped and we snuck into a **CIRCUS** to save her. Turns out she wasn't kidnapped, but Mom wanted to thank Steve for the thought.

As she said, 'It's the thought that counts.'

'Aww, cool!' Steve watched as I pulled out a container with a couple of slices of cake in it and handed it over to him. 'Let's eat it now!'

Steve opened the container, gave me one slice and pulled out the other slice of cake for himself.

Mmmm... **CAKE.**

'Your mom is the best,' Steve said, devouring the cake. 'Anyway, how's life going? Anything exciting happening in the world of Zack Zombie?'

'Eww, don't call me Zack. You know I don't like it! STEPHEN!'

'Dude... you know Stephen's not my name, right? I'm just Steve,' Steve laughed.

'Oh... well... you know what I mean. It's weird. Only my mom calls me Zack and only when she's **ANGRY.**' I shrugged.

Steve just laughed some more.

'But yeah, nothing too exciting happening. Endaria wrote me a letter from the Tundra Biome.'

'Oh man, the Boogieman Big Top Circus is in the Tundra Biome?! That's way cool,' Steve said before taking another bite of cake.

'Yeah, she said the equipment keeps freezing though, so that's a bit annoying. Also, I'm going on a school excursion tomorrow.'

'Whoa! I love **EXCURSIONS!** Human School hasn't let us go on an excursion since one of the kids almost got eaten by a Killer Bunny,' Steve said sadly.

'Why don't you come along on mine? You've perfected the art of mob disguise! You'd fit in perfectly!'

Steve grinned. 'Yeah! Where are you guys going?'

'The Mob Science Museum. And you know what that means...'

'ROCKETS!' Steve and I shouted at the same time.

'Okay, cool! This is gonna be so much fun. Just come in a **MOB**

DISGUISE. Oh, and here...' I started rummaging through my bag and pulled out a crumpled old school permission slip. 'Fill this in and sign it and give it to Ms. Bones when we're getting on the bus. I bet she won't even notice.'

'This is gonna be wicked!' Steve grinned. 'Rockets!'

TUESDAY

I was nervously waiting for Steve to show up out the front of Scare School this morning. I didn't tell the guys that Steve was going to **SNEAK** along cause they probably wouldn't be able to keep their cool.

Suddenly I saw a Skeleton limping towards us.

'Hi, team,' the Skeleton said in a chirpy voice. 'My name is Skoloo the Skeleton!'

'Hey, that's so weird! That sounds like my name!' Skelee waved at Skoloo. 'I'm Skelee the Skeleton!'

I tried so hard to hold in my laughter as everyone introduced themselves to Skoloo, or, as I knew him, Steve.

'Hey there, Skoloo. I'm Zombie. I think we're gonna have a great day.'

'Oh yeah! **ROCKETS!**' Skoloo fist pumped the air.

'Come on, everyone! On the bus!' Ms Bones called out, standing near the door with a clipboard.

As each kid passed her they either said their name if they had already handed in their permission slip, or handed over the signed slip.

The guys went in front of us, but Skoloo/Steve and I stayed a little further back. I let Steve stand in front of me and we shuffled forward slowly as the line progressed.

'Dude, that's a pretty wicked costume. How do you even do it?! You totally look **LEGIT.**'

'Thanks, man.' Steve grinned at me. 'Skeleton is my hardest one yet, but I'm pretty pleased with the turnout. **SKINS** are kinda fun to mod.'

When it was Steve's turn, he grinned at Ms. Bones as he handed her the permission slip.

If I could breathe, I'm sure I would have held my breath.

She didn't even look up as she snatched the paper from his bony fist and furiously scribbled something, then yelled, "NEXT."

Steve turned, gave me a wink and bounded onto the bus.

The bus ride to the Mob Science Museum was fun. The guys still had no clue that Skoloo was really Steve, and the longer he fooled them, the more fun we had.

When we got to the museum, Ms. Bones herded us off the bus and into the foyer. They made us sit on the floor while an ancient-looking Creeper gave us a talk.

'Back in my day...' the **PRE-CLASSIC** Creeper wheezed and took another breath, 'there were these creatures called...' another wheeze and breath, 'Humans.'

'Um, Mr. Creeper?' A Slime in the class put her hand up. 'There are still Humans around.'

'Oh?' The very old Creeper frowned. 'Well... they were really bad back in my day.'

'They're still **REALLY BAD!**' the Slime said again.

Steve sniggered next to me.

I elbowed him in the ribs while trying not to laugh.

'Well... Cranky Crispin the Creeper is going to take you round the museum now... don't touch anything,' the old Creeper wheezed. He turned to Cranky Crispin and said loudly, 'Watch that Slime. Talks too much. Never trust a mob kid that talks too much.'

The Slime just looked confused.

As we all stood and followed Cranky Crispin, Steve and I grinned at each other excitedly.

'Rockets?!'

'Rockets!'

'ROCKETS!'

'Dude, we've been here forever. Where are the rockets?!' Steve groaned at me.

He was right. Half the excursion had passed and all we'd seen were fake Pigs and Chickens and Biomes. We wanted rockets!

'And next up are the time-travelling rockets,' Cranky Crispin said with a **DEADPAN** voice.

'ROCKETS!' Steve and I shouted at the same time.

The class followed Cranky Crispin into a giant hall. The sides of the room were lined with big, old rockets. At the end of the hall was a giant rocket with dozens of spotlights on it, lighting it up from every direction.

We all walked to the end of the hall and stared at the giant rocket in amazement.

'This is our giant **TIME-TRAVELLING** rocket. This rocket

could maybe, possibly, under the right circumstances, maybe travel through time.' Cranky Crispin sounded like he was reading from a piece of paper. 'This rocket was designed by the best scientists the Overworld has to offer. It has never been tested or run in any official capacity.' Cranky Crispin stared at the class and sighed. '**DO NOT TOUCH.**'

Steve and I kept elbowing each other in excitement.

'Do you see the rocket?!'

'I see the rocket, do YOU see the rocket?!'

'It's a massive rocket!'

'Okay, class, now follow me.' Cranky Crispin led the class away from the giant rocket.

'Wait, that's it?!' I said in shock. 'We don't get to hear more about the rocket?!'

'Boo!' Steve frowned.

'Dude...' I grabbed Steve and we slowly dropped towards the back of the group. 'I have an **IDEA.**'

'What?' Steve asked.

'Just wait...' I said slowly.

Steve and I lingered at the back of the group until we were completely last. Then I waved at Steve to tell him to silently follow me.

We split off from the group and quietly made our way back to the massive rocket display.

'Dude, this rocket is amazing,' Steve whispered.

'Let's go in it!' I said excitedly, rubbing my hands together like an **EVIL VILLAIN.**

'What?' Steve said. 'I'm not so sure that's a good idea.'

'Come on, man! When will we ever get the opportunity again?! This is a rocket!'

'Oh, alright,' Steve agreed. A cheeky grin burst across his face. 'Let's do it!'

'Yes!' I pointed to a ladder leaning against the rocket. It led all the way to the top and into a **HATCH.** 'Let's go in there!'

Steve and I slowly climbed the ladder and rolled into the hatch at the top. I quickly pulled it shut so no one could see we were in there.

The cabin we were in looked like a pilot's cabin. There was a control panel with loads of buttons and switches everywhere. There were two seats and a tiny window.

I peeked out the window and saw the back of our class as they trailed out of the rocket hall and into the next room.

We were **ALONE** now.

'DUDE, THIS IS AMAZING!' Steve was bounding around the rocket, pressing buttons left and right.

'I KNOW!' I cackled with excitement. 'Hang on, Steve.

Do you... DO YOU WANNA SIMULATE A TAKE-OFF?!'

'DO I?!' Steve threw himself into one of the chairs and buckled in. I did the same in the chair next to him.

'Uh... **CAPTAIN ZOMBIE** reporting for duty, do you copy?' I pretended to talk into the microphone, with the transmission crackle and all.

'Captain Steve, also reporting for duty, over,' Steve answered into his microphone.

'Captain Steve and Zombie ready for take-off in 3... 2... 1... **BLAST-OFF!**'

'WHOO!' Steve cheered as we rattled around and pretended our rocket shot up into the air.

Suddenly I knocked a switch with my elbow while I was pretending to get thrown around as we pretend-blasted into outer space.

All of a sudden, there was a tremor.

'Zombie, what was that? What did you do? ' Steve asked looking around.

Then the tremor got bigger and louder.

Eventually the tremor was a roar. Everything was **SHAKING:** the control panel, all the buttons, the chairs and Steve and me.

'What is happening?!' I yelled at Steve over the roar. He couldn't hear me.

I looked out the window and realized that the hall was moving. Either that or...

We were moving!

THE ROCKET WAS TAKING OFF!

'STEVE!' I bellowed as loud as I could. 'WE'RE MOVING! WE'RE TAKING OFF! STEEEEEEVE!'

I got his attention and pointed out the window.

Steve's face went into a full-blown **PANIC.** I'd never seen a Skeleton face with that much expression.

Steve started frantically pressing all the buttons on the dashboard.

But nothing was stopping it now, the rocket was definitely **TAKING OFF.**

I just braced myself and looked out the tiny window as we shot out of the museum and into the sky.

Blast-off!

TUESDAY, LATER

It's okay. You're already dead. You can't get much worse than that, right?

I tried to calm myself down, but it wasn't really helping.

I heard muffled shouting from my side and turned to see Steve pointing at something out the window.

I squinted and saw a **BIG BLACK CIRCLE** with what looked like a swirling vortex around it.

'WHAT IS THAT?' I shouted at Steve.

I couldn't hear what he said.

Something about a 'back mole'? Why would Steve be talking about a mole on his back now?

Or maybe it was 'lack soul'? I mean, I know I'm **DEAD,** but it was a bit harsh to say I lack a soul.

I turned back to Steve and saw him shouting at me again.

'BLACK!! HOLE!!'

Oh. That makes sense.

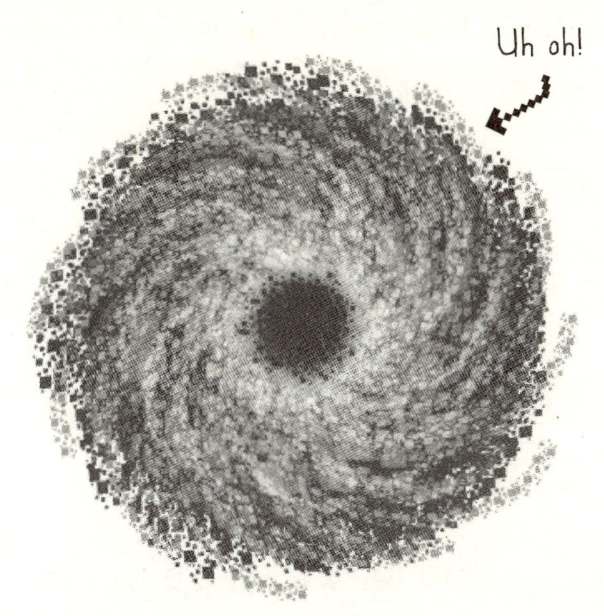

I suddenly realized what that meant: our rocket was getting sucked into a black hole.

'AGGGHHHH!!'

The moment we hit the black hole there was a weird, floaty feeling. Like gravity didn't exist anymore and if we weren't strapped in, we might have floated out of our seats.

POP!

Suddenly we were out the other side.

And gravity very much did exist.

We were **FALLING!**

'AAAGGGHHHHHH!' Steve and me screamed again as the rocket hurtled down.

TUESDAY, EVEN LATER

THUNK!!

The rocket stopped moving and everything went **DEAD SILENT.** I looked at Steve. He was still alive.

'Are you okay?' he asked me.

'Yeah,' I nodded.

Steve undid his seatbelt and looked out the window. 'Dude... we landed back in the museum. How?!'

'What?' I undid my seatbelt as well and scrambled over to look out the window with Steve.

He was right. We were back in the **EXACT SPOT** we had taken off from. The rocket was upright and everything. How...?

'WHAT ARE YOU TWO KIDS DOING UP THERE?' a cranky Blaze janitor yelled at us from below. That's weird. He was red. I'd never seen a red Blaze before. He must be REALLY mad.

'Yikes,' I said. 'Let's get outta here!'

Steve nodded and we scrambled down the ladder and bolted out of the room before the janitor could catch us or tell us off.

Running like mad, we skidded around a corner where we found our classmates standing around yet another **FAKE PIG.**

Phew! No one even noticed we were gone.

'And that's why Pigs can be controlled by a potato on a stick!' Cranky Crispin said happily.

Hang on...

'A potato on a stick...?' Steve turned to me with a confused look on his face. 'I thought it was a Carrot—'

'Next up! **MOOSHROOMS!**' our guide said, excited.

'Come along, kids,' a Skeleton in a tie said. 'You too, Zombie and Skoloo.'

'Who are you?' I asked.

'Very funny, Zombie. Top marks for that attempt. Now keep up with the group or it's detention for you.'

'MR. BONES!' one of the Endermen kids called out from the front of the group. 'I need to go to the bathroom.'

'Sure,' the Skeleton said and handed the kid a bathroom pass. 'Be quick.'

'Mr. Bones?!' I pulled Steve aside. 'Dude, what is happening? Where's Ms. Bones? Why is this guy acting like our teacher?'

'I dunno, man, but this is weird. Like, I can promise you that our tour guide was definitely not that **CHEERFUL** at the beginning of this tour.'

I turned to watch Cranky Crispin jump excitedly and smile with each question a mob kid called out.

'What happened to Cranky Crispin?'

'Cranky Crispin?' an Enderkid next to us cut in. 'That's mean. Don't be mean to Crafty Crispin. He's cool.'

Steve and I just looked at each other in shock. Neither of us knew what to say. What was going on?!

The tour of the museum finished and Mr. Bones herded us back onto the bus to return to school.

Steve and I were having a **SERIOUSLY WEIRD** time with Mr. Bones and the class. We just wanted to get away.

I tried to find Creepy, Skelee and Slimey but I couldn't see them anywhere.

'Mr. Bones!' I called out. 'I can't find Creepy, Skelee and Slimey. We must have left them behind!

We need to check the museum again.'

'Who?' Mr. Bones asked with a confused look on his face. 'Who are you talking about?'

'Creepy, Skelee and Slimey! You know them! They're my **FRIENDS.**'

A strange look crossed Mr. Bones' face and he knelt down to talk to me.

'I know that you feel lonely sometimes, Zombie. And making some friends up is fine, it really is.

But there's no need to pretend your imaginary friends got left in the museum. It's holding up our return to school.'

'**IMAGINARY** friends?!' I almost shouted.

'It's time to start being a bit more considerate. I'm glad you made a friend today in Skoloo, though.' Mr. Bones smiled, stood and walked back to the front of the bus. Without another glance at me, he smiled at the bus driver and told her we were good to go.

'We need to GET OUTTA HERE,' I stormed at Steve. 'Did you hear that? He just called me a loner with no friends! He thinks I made Creepy, Skelee and Slimey up!'

'Dude, something really weird is going on,' Steve said, and then he pointed out the bus window.

A Human and a Zombie were walking down the street together. They were just walking like two normal friends, **HANGING OUT.** Other mobs hopped and walked by and didn't blink an eye. They should all be running and screaming, but it was like no one cared that a Human was out and about!

'What the what?!' I turned to Steve. 'Let's go to my place and **TEST** this out.'

When I got home, I heard Mom and Dad in the kitchen.

'I'm home!' I called out nervously.

'Zombie!' Dad called out. 'We're in here!'

I turned to Steve and waved at him to stay there and not follow me in. He would be able to hear everything from the hallway anyway.

I walked into the kitchen and stopped dead in my tracks.

Well, I was dead anyway, but still.

Mom was slouched at the table with her feet up on a chair, playing a **GAME** on her phone.

Huh? I'd never seen her do that. Normally she was super busy organizing everything.

And Dad... Dad was at the crafting table.

COOKING.

And cooking something that smelled... good?

Whaaa...?! Dad has only ever cooked for us once, when Mom was away. He burnt the pancakes to a crisp and put blackstrap molasses instead of syrup on top. Eugh!

Dad had an apron tied around his waist and a wooden spoon in his hand. 'Son! How was the excursion? Tell me all about it.'

'Um, sure.' I nodded. 'We went to the Mob Science Museum and we had a tour guide named Cranky Crispin—I mean, Crafty Crispin. He showed us around.'

'That's good,' Dad nodded while stirring the big pot on the crafting table. 'Did you see the rocket?'

'Yup,' I gulped. 'Therocketwasgreat,' I speed whispered.

'What was that? I didn't hear that.'

'The rocket was great. **NOTHING HAPPENED.**'

'Oh, that's good. As long as you had a good time.'

I turned back to the hallway and saw Steve mouthing at me.

What was he saying?

He pointed at himself. Then at me. Then drew a circle with his hands. Or was it a **HEART?**

Finally he got frustrated and whispered, 'Ask if you have friends!'

What?

After my **PEA-SIZED** brain took a second to process this, I cottoned on. Mr. Bones mentioned that I had no friends and that Creepy, Skelee and Slimey didn't exist. I could test Dad and Mom and see if they remembered the guys.

I turned back to the kitchen. 'So, uh... I had a pretty good time at the museum.'

'Yes, so you said. I'm glad you enjoyed yourself, son.' Dad was still stirring the pot with laser focus.

'I, uh... made a **FRIEND.**'

Dad stopped stirring the pot. Mom put down her phone.

'Did you now?' Dad said excitedly. 'I'm so proud of you! Congratulations!'

'Yeah... thanks. Have I ever mentioned Creepy to you? Or Slimey? Or Skelee?'

'Of course you have!' Dad ruffled my head.

Phew! I was right! Maybe everyone at school was just being weird. Probably playing a prank on me for all those times I played pranks on them.

'They're your imaginary friends,' Mom said, before turning back to the game on her phone.

Wait, what?

'My what?'

'Oh sorry, right. I know you don't like us calling them that. Your, uh, **"LONG-DISTANCE"** friends.' Mom grinned at me.

I turned around, stormed back to the hallway and pulled Steve out of the house.

'Something very weird is going on. Everyone is **DIFFERENT.** And Creepy, Slimey and Skelee don't exist!'

WEDNESDAY

After that, we went to Steve's place and it was pretty much the same thing. After he changed out of his Skeleton skin, everyone knew him but things were weird. Stuff wasn't in the right place and everything was just a little bit... **OFF.**

So Steve and I went our separate ways to sleep in our own houses, but we agreed to skip school and meet up again tomorrow.

That is, today.

After a weird sleep, I met Steve in the park.

'Dude, what is going on?! Everything is just a little bit **WEIRD.**'

'I know!' Steve exclaimed. 'The Villagers I live with kept telling me stories about my parents. The real Villagers don't know anything about my parents! And they hate it when I ask! Something is definitely up.'

'Let's go back to the museum,' I said.

'That's where everything started getting weird.'

We managed to get into the museum for free cause Steve and I both still had our **WRISTBANDS** on from the excursion yesterday.

We stood in the foyer. 'Okay. Let's start at the beginning. We sat here while Cranky Crispin talked.

'No, it wasn't Cranky Crispin here. It was that other dinosaur of a Creeper. The one who looked about a thousand years old.'

'You're right! Then he handed us over to Cranky Crispin for the tour.' Steve and I retraced our steps through the museum. Everything seemed normal.

'Then we snuck into the rocket here.' Steve pointed at the big rocket.

'Okay, and then we went to the next room.' I started walking out of the rocket hall.

'**WAIT!**' Steve grabbed my arm to pull me back, but instead my arm just came off. 'Oh sorry. I forget that that happens.'

'That's alright,' I said. I took the arm from Steve and jammed it back into place. I gave my fingers a **WIGGLE** and then rotated the arm 360 degrees. 'Perfect.'

'What I was gonna say was, before we got out of the rocket, that strange red Blaze janitor saw us. Then we ran into the next room to catch up with class and that's when everything was suddenly different.'

'You're right!' I nodded. 'So something must have happened to everyone else while we were in the rocket.'

'Hey, I know you kids!' a grumpy voice shouted from behind us. 'You were the ones in the rocket!'

It was the **CRANKY,** red Blaze janitor from yesterday!

Busted!

I turned to run in the other direction, but before I could take a step, I was yanked back by a tug on my shirt.

'Hey, careful! This is my favorite shirt. I only have **THREE HUNDRED** just like it,' I grunted. We were caught and in trouble and my shirt was going to rip. Just great.

'I heard you kids talking about how things are different. Very different, but also... not very different?'

I squinted at the janitor in suspicion.

'Yes.'

'Well, I may have some information that might be useful to you.'

'Well, we don't need any information,' I grunted, as I tried to pull my shirt from the janitor's **FIERY** grasp.

'Wait, no, yes we do,' Steve cut me off. He turned to the smug-looking janitor. 'What do you know?'

'Why don't you tell me what *you* know instead?'

'I didn't spawn yesterday.' I glared at him.

Steve cut me off again. 'Well, you caught us in the rocket, so we got out, but after that everything got strange and weird—a little bit different. Like, some things are different, some people don't exist.'

'Well...' the Blaze scratched his chin thoughtfully. 'That ain't no regular rocket. That's a special rocket.'

'What do you mean **"SPECIAL"?**'

'Did you read the museum plaque about it?'

'No,' Steve and I answered at the same time.

'All we got told was that it was a time-travelling rocket and **"DO NOT TOUCH"**,' Steve explained.

'I reckon you should go read the plaque,' the janitor said, finally letting go of my shirt.

Steve and I ran over to the plaque sitting in front of the rocket.

This is the Omega M45A Rocket.

Although first designed to time travel, there was one flaw in this rocket that made it completely unusable. Every time the scientists tried to time travel with it, they ended up jumping into an **ALTERNATE UNIVERSE.** The machine had been incorrectly coded. This made the rocket completely useless for its intended purpose.

Because no one ever actually wants to travel to an alternate universe, the scientists donated it to the museum in a trade for a Golden Carrot and a stuffed Ocelot. They chose not to comment on what they did with the stuffed Ocelot.

'Dude...' Steve said slowly.

'I know. What in the Overworld would they want a dead Ocelot for?' I shook my head in confusion.

'NOT THAT!' Steve punched me in the arm. 'The rocket! It's not a time-travelling rocket, it's a dimension-travelling rocket! We didn't go through a black hole, we went through a **WORMHOLE!** We're in an alternate dimension!'

'Oh... oh no. Not again.' I paused. 'Wait, what's the difference between a black hole and a wormhole?'

'A black hole is a **DEAD END,** it just sucks everything into it. A wormhole is connected to something on the other side... like an alternate universe!' Steve said.

'Your friend is right,' the janitor said. 'It seems to me you mob kids have put the blocks together.'

'Well, we gotta try and get back! Come on,' I grabbed Steve by the arm and pulled him towards the rocket.

We were already climbing when the janitor yelled, 'That's not gonna work!'

We ignored him and climbed into the **PILOTS'** seats, strapping ourselves in.

'Uhh, do you remember how we accidentally set this off last time?' Steve asked.

'I don't know,' I looked around. 'I think I knocked that stick with my elbow.'

Steve shrugged. 'Give it a go.'

I pushed it to the left. Nothing happened. I pushed it to the right.

Still nothing.

I wiggled the stick around like a **JOYSTICK** but the rocket didn't move.

Not even a tiny tremor.

'I told you it's not going to work!' I heard the janitor call from below.

'You're not being helpful!' I yelled.

I turned back to the console and started smashing every button I could find, but nothing was working.

Eventually Steve and I just sat there, staring at the dead console. Then he turned to me, 'Maybe we should ask the janitor for help? I think he knows something.'

I swallowed my **PRIDE** and nodded. 'But you do it.'

Steve rolled his eyes, opened the rocket window and stuck his head out. 'Um... Mr. Janitor. Do you know how we get this rocket going so we can go back to our own dimension?'

'Why, yes, I think I do,' I heard his voice echo up to us.

Steve pulled his head back in. 'Zombie, I think we need to go down.'

'**URGH.**' I nodded and unbuckled my seatbelt.

Steve and I climbed out of the rocket, and went down to meet the janitor.

The janitor looked smug. 'Finally ready to listen, are we?'

I didn't say anything, but Steve nodded.

'How do we get outta here? You clearly know something. You gotta help us,' Steve said.

'I don't have to help you.' The janitor paused dramatically. 'But I will. Cause I'm **NICE** like that. I don't know how to get the rocket working again.'

I groaned in frustration.

'But I know someone who does.'

'Wait, what? Who?' Steve asked.

'It'll be hard finding her. But it'll be worth it. She knows everything about everything.'

'Who?'

The janitor gulped. 'I would go with a gift, if I were you. She can be quite... **SNAPPY.** But if anyone can get you out of here, it'll be her.

'WHO?!' Steve and I yelled at the same time.

'The Wandering Witch.'

THURSDAY

Steve and I weren't particularly happy about having to go find a Witch, but there wasn't much we could do about it.

Plus, yesterday, after making plans to meet up again today, I went home and realized something.

WESLEY didn't exist in this universe.

I'm an only child.

Which I enjoyed for like five minutes.

But it turns out, I kinda like Wesley. And being an only child means Mom and Dad pay a lot of attention to me. Like... way too much.

I needed Wesley back.

So today, Steve and I were trudging through the forest, looking for the **WANDERING WITCH.**

The only problem was, the janitor didn't really give us any specific details or directions. He just said to go into the forest and when we got to the **MIDDLE** to yell her name three times.

'Does this feel like the middle of the forest to you?' Steve asked.

The Wandering Witch's home turf

'I really have no idea,' I said. 'It feels like we've been walking for ages, but I also hate walking. Don't you think it's weird that the Witch lives in a **FOREST**, not a swamp?'

'Yeah,' Steve nodded. 'But that might be part of the alternate dimension.

Maybe Witches live in forests here, not swamps.'

'Maybe they're really nice and helpful here too! I mean, Glenda is super nice even though she is scary,' I offered.

Steve snorted with laughter. 'We'll see.'

Suddenly Steve stopped. There was a big **BOULDER** in front of him and he climbed it. 'This is it,' he said. 'This is the middle of the forest.'

'Okay,' I shrugged. I had no idea, so if Steve said so, I wasn't going to argue.

Steve held his hand out to me and helped pull me onto the rock. 'Okay, three times, Zombie, got it?'

I nodded.

Steve took a deep breath and then we chanted, '*Wandering Witch. Wandering Witch. Wandering Witch.*'

We paused.

Nothing happened.

'Huh,' Steve said slowly. 'Maybe it takes some time for the call to reach her.'

'Maybe the janitor lied and sent us on a wild **PARROT** chase,' I suggested.

'Wait, shhh. Did you hear that?'

I paused and listened.

There was a rustling sound in the trees. It sounded too close to be the wind. Something was making those trees rustle.

'W-W-W-Wandering W-Witch? Is that you?' I asked.

'YES!' An ugly Witch **LEAPT** out of the bushes and into the clearing in front of us.

'AAAGGGHHHHH!!!' Steve and I screamed at the same time.

'HAHAHAHA,' the Witch cackled. 'They **NEVER** expect it!'

Scared us half to life!

Steve and I stopped clutching each other as we watched the Witch double over with laughter.

Then she stood, wiping tears from her eyes. 'So, what did you want?'

'Uhh...'

'Um...'

'Come on! Out with it!' The Witch started tapping her foot.

'We're in the **WRONG** dimension!'

'You mean Biome.' The Witch rolled her eyes. 'That's not my problem. There are easy ways to travel between Biomes, you can figure it out.' Then she turned to walk away.

'NO, WAIT! PLEASE!' I yelled out. 'We're in the wrong **DIMENSION**, really. We got into a rocket and accidentally travelled to this alternate dimension and we need to go back to our own dimension.'

The Witch paused. 'Do you really...?' She spun around on one heel and stomped back to us. 'Name one thing that's different between this dimension and yours.'

'Uh, my little brother—'

The Witch held a hand up to my face to stop me. 'I meant, give me an example I care about.'

'Well, um...'

'Witches live in **SWAMPS** in our dimension,' Steve offered.

'Oh really?' The Witch smiled. 'I always liked swamps. ALRIGHT, FOLLOW ME!' Suddenly, she spun around on her heel and stomped away.

Steve and I scrambled off the boulder and sped after her.

We followed the Wandering Witch through the forest until we reached a small hut with a moat and a water wheel. Smoke flowed out of the chimney and there were flowers everywhere.

Basically it looked like the Witch had stolen a **FAIRYTALE COTTAGE.**

'This can't be hers... right?' I mumbled to Steve.

Steve's face was scrunched up in confusion. 'No. Way.'

We followed the Witch as she slammed open the front door and plopped down at the table in the kitchen.

The inside of the hut was just as confusing as the outside. It was **CUTE AND COSY.**

Exactly the kind of place Witches from our dimension would *hate*.

'Tell me more,' the Witch said. She waved her hand and a teapot floated out of nowhere and poured her a cup of tea.

She didn't ask if we wanted anything, but we probably wouldn't have said yes anyway. Never trust a Witch.

Steve explained the whole thing. How we went on a school excursion, snuck into a rocket and everything that had happened since then, including the janitor who told us about her.

'He's right. I can help you. Well, not directly, but I know how you can help yourselves.' She sipped her tea.

We waited.

She **SIPPED** again.

Steve held his breath.

The Witch dunked a biscuit in her tea.

Finally she said, 'But nothing in this Overworld is given for nothing.'

'What does that mean?' I hissed to Steve.

'Oh, the gift!' Steve remembered. He turned back to the Witch. 'We have something for you that may help you remember.'

He handed her a box.

The Wandering Witch acted surprised. 'Oh, you shouldn't have,' she said as she grabbed the box. She opened it to find **SPIDERS' EYES.** 'Amazing.'

She shut the box and turned back to Steve and me. 'Yes, I think you have earned the right to know how to free yourself from this dimension. Although I don't think it's so bad.'

I kept my mouth **SHUT.** I didn't think the Witch would want to hear what I had to say about this dimension.

'If you want to leave this dimension, you must do it the same way you came in: in that rocket.'

'But we tried that!' I said. Steve stomped on my foot under the table and the Witch glared at me.

Oww.

'I wasn't finished. Anyway, you must return from that which you came, which is the rocket. But to return to your dimension, you need a clear blue crystal: **LAPIS LAZULI.'**

'But,' the Witch continued, 'Lapis Lazuli can be mined in one place and one place only. **THE MAZE OF FIRE.'**

I gulped.

The Witch continued, 'The Maze of Fire isn't actually on fire, but it is very difficult and full of terrors. Only the bravest mobs would even attempt it. Once you reach the center of the maze, you will find the entrance to a cave. You needn't go into the cave. The Crystal may be mined from the walls of the entrance. Once you find the Lapis Lazuli, call my name three times and I will help you leave the maze.'

'Hang on, if you can swoop in and out of the maze, why can't you just swoop us right in there. Why do we have to go through the whole thing?' I asked.

'Haven't you ever **EARNED** anything in your life?' she snapped at me. 'Now leave before I change my mind and refuse to help you leave the maze.'

Steve and I stood.

'Wait,' Steve said. 'Where is the Maze of Fire?'

'That way.' The Witch pointed behind her and turned away to stoke her fire. 'Call me when you have the **CRYSTAL** and not a moment before. I don't appreciate mobs that waste my time.'

Steve and I just looked at each other, then we left the Witch's cozy hut.

I guess we were going to the Maze of Fire.

FRIDAY

'This maze is huge!' I couldn't believe my **EYEHOLES.**

Steve frowned.

After we'd left the Witch's hut yesterday, it had been too late to go maze hunting. So we'd gone home to eat and sleep, so we'd be all ready for today. But we had spent ages walking 'that way' (where the Witch had pointed) and had only just found the maze. And now the maze was HUGE!

'It's a **HEDGE MAZE,'** Steve said.

The hedges were the height of two adult Zombies and the width of a Zombie lying down. The entrance was dark and creepy.

'Maybe I should wait for you here?' I suggested.

Steve glared and then whacked me on the arm. 'If I'm going in that maze, you are too.'

I sighed. 'Well, when do we go in? Like, now?'

'Why would we wait?' Steve asked.

'I dunno, I feel like there should be a "ready, set, go" moment.'

Steve rolled his eyes, grabbed me by the sleeve and dragged me forward.

As we entered the maze, we heard a warning DA-DONG.

'How bad can it be?' Steve asked. I'm a Human, you're a Zombie. We're technically each other's worst **DAYMARE.** It can only get better, right?'

'Sure,' I nodded.

I didn't think disagreeing with him was going to help either of us at this point. The Maze of Fire didn't need fire to be **SCARY** at all.

We walked through the maze in silence for a bit before I had a thought.

'Did the Wandering Witch say what the Lapis Lazuli was for?' I asked.

'Uhh, I don't think so.' Steve shook his head.

'I hope she didn't just send us here to get rid of us,' I said.

'I dunno, dude.' Steve shook his head. 'If the Witch's hut is anything to go by, she seems super different to the Witches in our dimension. She liked the Spiders' eyes and I think she wanted to be helpful. I think—

WATCH OUT!'

Steve grabbed me by the back of my shirt and yanked me back.

Man, I'm going to need a new shirt.

'What was that for?!'

'LOOK!' Steve pointed ahead of us.

There was a drop-off. It wasn't a big drop-off, maybe a bit shorter than me. It wouldn't have been the end of the world if I'd walked right off it.

'Dude, it's just a **LEDGE.**'

Steve rolled his eyes. 'Look *properly*.'

I walked closer to the ledge and looked again.

Oh.

It wasn't the ledge Steve had pulled me back from.

It was the lake that gently lapped at the bottom of it. Water makes us Zombies grow white skin—super **ITCHY.** But that's not the worst of it—the worst is we turn into Drowned if we are in there too long.

'Oh, right. Yeah, that would have been bad.' I shuddered. 'Thanks, Steve.'

Steve shrugged it off. 'We need to find a way around it.'

I looked from side to side and realized the lake took up the entire width of the path in the maze.

'Hang on,' I said aloud. 'Why is there a **LAKE** in the maze?'

Steve paused. 'I have no idea. To throw us off, I suppose. Anyway, I don't think there's a way around it. The lake takes up all this space and it goes for ages. Can we maybe climb the hedge?

We might be able to climb around the lake?' Steve suggested.

I walked to the hedge that lined the path, jumped and grabbed at a branch in the hedge. As soon as I touched the hedge, it turned into smooth blocks. No hand holds at all.

'Urgh!' I turned back to Steve and shook my head.

'Maybe we can make a **RAFT** out of something?' Steve suggested.

We both looked around. There was nothing now that the hedges were block walls.

I looked at the water again.

It was dark and creepy.

'Maybe I can just wait here?' I suggested.

'Stop trying to get out of this,' Steve said.

He kept wandering around trying to find something to help us. 'How would I go on without you anyway?'

'Well, you could **SWIM** it, couldn't you?'

Steve stopped. 'I suppose I could.' He grabbed a Stone lying on the ground and threw it into the lake.

It landed with a soft plop and sank.

'Well, it doesn't look like there is anything in there,' Steve said slowly.

'Yes! You can swim ahead and I'll wait here,' I said.

'Yes, I can swim... and you can sit on my back while I swim.'

'Yes—wait, what?' I turned around to face Steve. 'Uh, no. That sounds like a bad idea. I'm too heavy, I'll **SINK** you.'

'No, you won't. Come on.' Steve turned and started slowly shuffling his way down the ledge until he was at the edge of the water. He dipped his toe in and then turned to smile at me.

'This is perfect water for swimming!'

I grimaced and slowly followed until I was standing beside him.

'Okay, I'm going to get into the water and you sit on my back. Then we'll swim across!'

'I still think this is a **BAD IDEA,**' I said, but Steve didn't seem to hear me. Or he ignored me.

Steve lay down in the water, face down. Then he quickly popped his head up and said, 'By the way, I can't hold my breath like this forever.

As soon as I put my head down, get on my back and tap my shoulder and I'll start swimming, okay?'

I **FROWNED,** but Steve put his face down into the water, so I had no choice but to step onto his back, trying really hard not to touch any water.

Urgh, water!

I was standing on his back trying to work out how to sit without any water getting on me when Steve lifted his head, gasped for some air and then started swimming.

While I was **STILL STANDING** on his back!

I hated every second of it, but I didn't want to make Steve stop in case we both lost our balance and I fell off into the water.

I glanced at the dark water and shuddered.

Nope, I would much rather be up here.

Using Steve as a **SURFBOARD.**

Steve swam easily through the water—he almost seemed to be enjoying himself.

I only started enjoying myself when I could see the shore again!

As soon as Steve reached the sandy beach, I jumped off his back and kissed the ground in relief. Oh, how I'd missed solid ground.

Steve stood up, water dripping off of him. 'Dude, were you **SURFING** me?! That was so much fun! We should do it again!'

'Never,' I groaned, lying flat on the ground. I didn't want to move.

'Uh, Zombie?'

'I don't wanna move. Give me a second to enjoy the solid ground again.'

'Nope, you gotta move. YOU GOTTA MOVE NOW!' Steve yelled.

I looked up and saw a swarm of Spiders scuttling towards me.

And not just any Spiders.

CAVE SPIDERS.

FRIDAY, LATER

'RUUUUUNN!!!!' Steve yelled.

I had already jumped up and turned to run when I realized that I couldn't.

There was **NOWHERE TO GO.**

The lake was behind me and the Spiders were in front of me. The sides were walled off by the hedges.

Steve was wading into the water again.

He turned and saw me standing there, **STUCK.**

He ran back to me. 'Zombie, hop on my shoulders, quick!'

I really didn't want to go back into the water, but I had no choice. I awkwardly climbed onto Steve's shoulders and he waded into the water.

Just in time too, because as we turned around, the Cave Spiders reached the edge of the water.

'Oh man, what do we do?!' I cried.

'Those are Cave Spiders! What are they doing outside a **CAVE?!**'

'They must have come from the cave where the Lapis Lazuli is. We must be close,' Steve said calmly.

'How are you so calm?!'

'It's fine, we'll—hang on.' Steve stopped mid-sentence and craned his neck back to look up at me. 'What are you doing?'

'Uh, trying not to touch the water. What are you doing?'

'Zombie... you're a mob. Your kind literally ride Spiders.'

'Not exactly my kind. Skeletons are **SPIDER JOCKEYS,** usually,' I said.

Steve face-palmed at my response. 'My point is... Spiders don't attack you. They only attack Humans! That's why I ran away! Why did you run away?!'

'I dunno,' I said, embarrassed. 'I guess I forgot Spiders don't attack me. I got caught up in the moment. You were screaming **"RUN",** so I ran.'

'Come on, then. We need to figure out a way to swap.'

'Swap?' I asked.

'Yeah, swap. I'll climb on your shoulders and you can walk through the Spiders,' Steve said.

'How long can you be in the water?'

'Um, about thirty seconds before I turn into a **DROWNED.**'

'Okay, timer starts now!' Steve suddenly dropped me into the shallow water.

'AAAGGGHHHHHH!!!' I screamed as my feet hit the water. My trademark filth started to wash away. 'NOOO!!!'

Steve ignored my cries and clambered onto my back and then up onto my shoulders.

'COME ON, GO!' Steve yelled.

I ran out of the water and shook my feet, trying to get all the droplets off. I was too late. I stared in **HORROR** at my legs. I had beautifully disgusting legs down to my ankles. Then my feet were a clean white color where the skin had regrown. Yuck.

'Zombie...' Steve whispered nervously.

It was then I remembered the Spiders. They were surrounding us.

But when I stepped forward, the Spiders parted way for me.

Steve sighed in relief as I took another step forward.

But then from beside me, one **JUMPED** up at Steve. He was too high up on my shoulders, so the Spider missed, but then they all started jumping to try and get him. Lucky they weren't giant Spiders!

'Zombie, can you walk a little faster? I don't wanna give these guys too much practice at jumping at me! One of them might make it!' Steve hissed.

'Oh, right.' I started walking a little faster. The Spiders still opened up and made way for me, but it didn't take long for us to realize that the Spiders were **FOLLOWING** us.

'What do we do?!' I asked Steve.

'I dunno! I didn't think this far.'

'We need to get rid of them, but how? Oh wait, which way?' I suddenly realized I'd come to a fork in the path. 'Left or right?'

'Oh man... which way do the Spiders want to go?' Steve said.

'We're asking the Spiders now?'

'Well, they're Cave Spiders! They must have come from a cave!'

I looked down and asked the **SWARM** of Spiders, 'Which way should I take to get to the cave?'

They didn't answer. Of course they didn't answer, they're Spiders.

'Maybe we should go left?'

'Look!' Steve pointed down from his spot on my shoulders.

The Spiders weren't surrounding us anymore. They had started scuttling down the right fork in the path.

'That has gotta be the way to the cave,' Steve said. 'Why else would they just leave us?'

I shrugged, jostling Steve.

We waited until all the Spiders had left, then we followed them from a safe distance. Eventually, we reached a small clearing surrounded by hedges. We were in the center of the maze!

FRIDAY, EVEN LATER

'Look!' I whispered. In the middle of the clearing was a small, dark cave. And just past the entrance to the cave, before the path dropped down, there was something **SPARKLY AND BLUE** shining out from behind some rocks. 'That must be the Lapis Lazuli Crystal!'

I ran towards it, but suddenly Steve screamed.

Out of nowhere, a Shulker appeared!

With no warning, it started firing projectiles at us!

Steve leaped off my shoulders and pulled out a **SWORD** from his inventory. 'GO GET THE CRYSTAL! I'll deal with this guy!' Steve turned to the Shulker and started dodging, trying to get close enough to stop it.

I only wasted a second watching Steve, then I grabbed a **PICKAXE** from his inventory and ran towards the cave.

It was the Lapis Lazuli sparkling, so I started hammering away. After three whacks of the Pickaxe, I started panting. After five, I was exhausted.

'ZOMBIE! HURRY UP!' Steve yelled from behind me.

I turned and saw Steve battling it out. He was lunging from side to side with speed.

I turned back to the Crystal in the wall. 'I'm gonna get you if it **RE-KILLS** me!' I yelled, and started crashing the Pickaxe into the rock with new energy.

Before I knew it, more than half the Crystal was free and I started tugging at it with my hands.

After a few more goes, it yanked free and I fell backwards. I rolled and suddenly I was teetering on the edge of the steep slope down into the cave.

'AAAAGGHHH!!' I scrambled back. That was a close one!

I ran out of the cave and saw Steve and the **SHULKER** still fighting.

'I've got it!' I yelled out.

'THEN CALL...'

THWACK!

'THE WITCH!'

THWACK!

I gripped the Lapis Lazuli tightly, shut my eyes and yelled out, 'WANDERING WITCH! WANDERING WITCH! WANDERING WITCH!'

I opened my eyes but nothing had happened.

SWOOSH!

Suddenly the Wandering Witch appeared on a broomstick.

'What have we here?' she cackled.

I don't know why she cackled, nothing about this was funny.

'Hop on, kiddos!'

Instead, I ran straight past the Witch, towards the Shulker. The Shulker had its back to me so I leaped on top of it, using my weight to slam its shell closed.

Steve turned and bolted out of there towards the Witch and her hovering broom, and I was right behind him.

'Where's the Lapis Lazuli?' she yelled at us.

I held the Crystal up, and she allowed us to jump on the broomstick.

Just as she kicked off the ground, the Shulker reopened and started firing **PROJECTILES** again.

But the Witch used her broomstick to dodge and then we were out of range. Phew!

We flew high into the sky, the three of us and the precious Lapis Lazuli, away from the Maze of Fire.

Eventually we landed back in front of the museum.

'Thanks for helping us and giving us a lift,' Steve said.

'Nothing in life is **FREE**, you know, kiddo.'

'Oh man, we should have known,' I groaned.

'It's not much. All I want is for you to tell Boris that Willow likes Mooshroom stew.'

'Who's Boris?' I asked.

She frowned at me. 'Boris, you ridiculous Zombie, is the Blaze janitor who sent you to me. I can't believe you didn't even ask his name before you asked him for help. **RUDE!** I bet you don't even know my name.'

Steve and I scoffed and laughed. 'Of course we know your name!' I laughed. 'It's Wandering Witch!'

'That's not my name!' she said.

I turned to Steve and we both had panicked looks on our faces. 'It's not?'

'No! That'd be like saying your name is Zombie just because you're a Zombie,' she scolded.

I looked confused. 'But my name is **ZOMBIE.**'

'Oh, never mind,' she snapped. 'Just tell Boris that Willow likes Mooshroom stew.' Then before we could say anything she kicked up and off the ground, and flew away.

'Wait!' I yelled. 'You didn't tell us how to use the Lapis Lazuli!'

She **CACKLED.**

FRIDAY, EVEN LATER STILL

'I don't think she's coming back,' I said out loud.

'I think we kind of deserved that,' Steve admitted.

I hated to agree, but I agreed. 'Also, what does that even mean, "Willow likes Mooshroom stew"?'

'Maybe it's a CODE?' Steve suggested.

'I dunno.' I shrugged. 'Maybe Boris will know how to use the Lapis Lazuli,' I said.

We walked up to the front door of the museum, but when I pulled on the handle it stayed shut. I pulled harder but it wouldn't open.

'Zombie, they're **CLOSED!**'

'What?' I turned and saw Steve standing next to a sign with the museum's opening hours on it.

'They're closed!'

'Well, I'm not waiting a moment longer than I have to!' I marched around to the side of the building and found a window. 'Steve! Come here!'

Steve followed me around the corner and found me staring upwards. 'I think I can guess,' he said.

'Great,' I said. 'Come on, then.'

Steve knelt down and I got onto his shoulders. When he stood, I was at a perfect height to **SHIMMY** the window up.

Once it was open enough, I clambered through and clattered to the floor.

I looked around and realized I was in an office of some type. There was a desk and a chair and a bunch of papers, but nothing interesting.

I poked my head out the window and called down to Steve, 'One minute, I'll find something to pull you up with.'

I went into the next room and jumped when I saw an **OCELOT** staring at me.

Oh, wait. It was stuffed.

Hmmm, where had I heard about a **STUFFED** Ocelot recently?

Oh well.

I dragged it back to the office and dangled it out the window. 'Grab onto the tail, Steve!' I was gripping its dry, stiff paws.

'Gross,' Steve said, but he jumped and caught the Ocelot's **TAIL.**

I heaved and just managed to pull the Ocelot, and Steve, back through the window.

Finally, we were all sitting in the office. Me, Steve and the Ocelot.

'Alright! Now, we just gotta find that rocket!' I said.

Turns out, finding the rocket didn't take long at all. The museum layout was exactly as we remembered and this was technically our third visit.

As we bounded into the rocket hall, we ran smack into Boris the red Blaze, who was mopping the floor.

'BORIS!' I yelled. 'We got it!'

'Huh? Oh, you kids! What're you doing here? The museum is closed!'

'But we need to get back to our own dimension! We don't have time to wait for the museum to open,' Steve said.

'Plus, we'd be sneaking into the rocket whether the museum was open or closed,' I added. 'But Boris, we have the Lapis Lazuli! Look!' I proudly held up the clear blue CRYSTAL.

'Oh cool,' he said. 'What does it do?'

'Uh...' I looked at Steve. 'We actually don't know. Do you know by any chance?'

Boris shook his head.

I sighed. 'That's alright. We'll figure it out. Come on, Steve!' I started heading towards the rocket.

'Oh, by the way,' Steve said. 'The Wandering Witch told us to tell you that Willow likes Mooshroom stew.'

'Oh, does she?' Boris lit up.

LITERALLY... he's a Blaze.

'Uh, okay,' Steve said, before turning and following me to the rocket. 'I don't know what kinda code that was, but I think he's happy.'

I shrugged, then climbed the ladder and clambered in through the hatch.

I strapped myself in and Steve did the same. Then I held up the Lapis Lazuli.

'Okay, this Crystal must go somewhere. We just gotta work out where,' I said.

We looked in every part of the **CONSOLE.** But there were hundreds of buttons and switches cluttering every block, making it almost impossible to tell things apart.

When I leant down to check underneath the console, I accidentally knocked a lever and suddenly the rocket started shaking.

'IS THIS HAPPENING?' Steve yelled with happiness.

'YEAH!!' I held the Lapis Lazuli up as the rocket roared to life and started shaking. **'LET'S GO HOME!'**

LAST TUESDAY (YEP, THAT'S RIGHT)

After a few minutes of the rocket shaking, it suddenly stopped again.

'Is it done already?' I asked.

Steve shrugged and looked out the window.

Suddenly a croaky voice starting yelling. 'What're you kids doing?! Get outta there before I call your parents! That ain't no **TOY!**'

I looked out the window and saw a cranky Blaze janitor yelling at us.

But it clearly wasn't Boris. At least, not the Boris we knew. This Blaze was a normal **YELLOW** color.

Steve and I grinned and high-fived each other.

I started to climb out of the rocket but then Steve called out, 'Wait! I need to put my **SKOLOO** skin mod back on!'

I threw my head back and laughed. 'I totally forgot about that. That would have been great, walking into the museum with a Human. I guess that was one good thing about the other dimension. Humans and Zombies could just be friends.'

'Yeah,' Steve nodded as he perfected his costume. 'Okay, ready to go.'

Then we clamored out of the rocket and darted right past **NOT-BORIS.**

'By the way, Mr. Janitor! Willow likes Mooshroom stew!' I shouted as I scurried by, then I turned and lobbed him the Lapis Lazuli.

'What?! How do you know Willow, the Stay-At-Home Witch?! And how do you know I'm making her dinner?' not-Boris called after me. 'And what's *this* for?' I heard him wonder as we left him behind, holding the clear, blue Crystal.

We skidded around a corner and ran smack into Ms Bones.

'Where have you two been?' she scolded. 'Go take your place with the other mob kids before I give you both **DETENTION** for sneaking off.'

Steve and I both dropped our heads to hide our grins and slunk over to join the group.

Then I spotted Creepy, Skelee and Slimey. 'Oh man,' I crowded near them. 'It's so good to have you guys back!'

'Back? I saw you, like, **TEN MINUTES** ago.' Creepy said, confused.

'Haha, don't worry.' I shook my head and hugged him.

BRRR, BRRR.

Huh? I jammed my hand into my pocket and pulled out a mobile phone. Oh, that's right—Mom told me to take it with me since I was going to be out on a school excursion. Hmm... wonder if it would have worked in the alternate dimension? Oh well.

It was a **TEXT:**

> Plz pick up ur brother from
> Pre-Scare School on ur way home.
> Love, Mom.

Wesley was back! And Mom was organized again!

Phew!

Ms. Bones frowned at me and pointed back at the tour guide.

'And this is a stuffed Ocelot,' Cranky Crispin grumbled as he gestured at a stiff Ocelot. 'We traded several of these for the rocket we just saw. Moving on...'

Steve and I laughed.

WE WERE BACK!